Jay Conrad Levinson About *More Power!*

"When I was in the middle of writing my first book, I said to my wife, 'you know, while writing this book, I have a feeling that's very unusual for me, yet feels very comfortable and right. I feel as though God is flowing through me with everything I write. My wife asked if that means I feel that I am God. I said that "I do not, but I do feel as though what I write is not something that I have learned but something that I just know.

So it is with Bob Bare's incredible book. While reading it, you get the unmistakable sense of not having to learn anything but simply tap into the timeless power that it already within you, just waiting for you to share with the planet.

That book I was writing, led to a tsunami of power that has thus far enlightened more than 30 million people. You can do the same if only you read Bob's clarification of the pathway, to truths that you know, you need to know, and you already possess."

Jay Conrad Levinson
The Father of Guerrilla Marketing
Author, "Guerrilla Marketing" series of books
The best known marketing brand in history
Named one of the 100 best business books ever written
Over 21 million sold; now in 63 languages

"Bob's extensive knowledge of business as a serial entrepreneur has allowed him to craft a powerful guide to business success. Bob shares his struggles as well as his successes, teaches you how to get into action and, ultimately, how to accurately measure your business growth."

Ursula Mentjes
Bestselling Author,
Selling with Intention
SalesCoachNow.com

More Power

An Entrepreneur's Roadmap to Success

BOB BARE

NEW YORK

More Power

An Entrepreneur's Roadmap to Success

ISBN 978-1-61448-270-3 paperback
ISBN 978-1-61448-271-0 eBook
Library of Congress Control Number: 2012935391

Morgan James Publishing
The Entrepreneurial Publisher
5 Penn Plaza, 23rd Floor,
New York City, New York 10001
(212) 655-5470 office • (516) 908-4496 fax
www.MorganJamesPublishing.com

Illustrations by:
Marcia Hill

Cover Design by:
Rachel Lopez
www.r2cdesign.com

Interior Design by:
Bonnie Bushman
bonnie@caboodlegraphics.com

This book is dedicated to three separate groups that I am very familiar with. The first are entrepreneurs everywhere, who keep the world functioning regardless of undeserved disdain they sometimes receive, and in spite of the hardships they often endure. Next are the spouses and significant others that sometimes feel like they are taking second place to a vision and dream, who hopefully learn how to endure and survive sharing their lives with their partner's vision and the trials that sometimes brings. Finally, I salute the children and family members of entrepreneurs, who may not have the same temperament and may not understand what drives their loved one's quest. Thank you for sharing your life with those of us who are marching to the creative and visionary drummer that drives entrepreneurs.

Contents

Foreword

For decades, I have studied the psychology of entrepreneurship. Through my bestselling books, coaching programs and live events, I have mentored tens of thousands of entrepreneurs around the world. Their passion, creativity, vision and seemingly unbreakable determination are an inspiration to me and constitute the keys to growth of our economy—and our country.

While highly skilled and motivated, many entrepreneurs lack the knowledge, the tools and the strategies it takes to make a business successful. I am passionate about teaching the infallible principles that allow entrepreneurs to design a profitable business that is aligned with their vision, allows them to enjoy life and generates immediate, yet consistent and sustainable wealth.

More Power! provides a blueprint that clearly delineates the science of entrepreneurial success in today's environment. Bob Bare draws from his 40 years of experience as a serial entrepreneur. Since his teenage years, Bob has studied and put into action proven strategies for immediate cash flow and lasting business success.

But Bob's achievements are not merely measured by a multimillion-dollar business created, grown and turned around. His ability to stay on track, true to his values and in line with his ultimate vision is what truly resonates with me. Bob shares my philosophy that there is a fast path to cash, a formula that guarantees:

1. Regular Increasing Cash Flow
2. Business Protection
3. Accelerated Growth
4. Cost and Risk Reduction
5. Effective Exit Strategy

In this easy yet powerful read, Bob shares insights to get you started or get you going on areas such as branding and identity, marketing, sales, business organization and structure, financing, media, targeting, competition, and many other fundamental aspects of business development.

Because like me, Bob is driven by a desire to pay it forward, and because I have mentored him myself through many of my programs, including Big Table, I know that the principles, strategies and insights contained in *More Power!*, when put to work, will result in a massive shift in your business, and improvements will be tangible and measurable.

Pay careful attention to the action steps, calendar them and discipline yourself to execute them. Don't get trapped in "Paralysis by Analysis." Your fear to play big doesn't serve you or anyone.

Robert Schuller once said "Better to do something imperfectly than to do nothing flawlessly."

You must implement the ideas in order to move forward, using your vision and your values as your compass and guides.

Everything you choose to do—or not to, impacts your business...and your life. By deciding to invest in learning from expert trainers and visionaries, you will make your vision your reality.

I challenge you to implement these principles...and Play the Biggest Game of Your Life...NOW!

—Loral Langemeier
Best selling author, internationally
acclaimed speaker, and expert money coach.

Acknowledgements

Sincere thanks to the many hours Robin Swindle (my first born and now my project manager) has devoted to editing, merging versions, and putting up with multiple changes to see this book completed.

Thanks to Elayna Fernandez, my friend and also branding and social media mentor, who has given invaluable guidance and taught me the importance of building a platform and staying true to my vision at the same time.

I appreciate Odell Stunkard for taking over the many tasks of running my businesses during the time I have worked on writing this book.

A big thank you to the team at BestSellingExperts.com for all the hours of ideas and work. Thank you Andrea, Taylor, Johnnie, Kenneth, Ernie, Annie, Connie, and again Odell, Robin, and Elayna for your loyalty and support.

Many thanks to my mentors who have taught me so much over the years, including Kenneth McCarthy, who taught me internet marketing and was an example of integrity. Rich Allen, who turned the principles of metrics from theory into reality. Loral Langemeier, who taught me the power of yes-energy and continues to coach my speaking and presentations. Pastor Tony Hoult, who is always a supporter and encourager.

Thanks to Rick Frishman of AuthorUniversity, David Hancock of Morgan James Publishing, and Jay Conrad Levinson for helping me complete what I began.

Thanks to my wife Jan, who supported all the expense and travel and time alone while I walked the path of an entrepreneur, and as I attended the many conferences and seminars to learn and grow, from our first business together 37 years ago to our continuing adventures today.

Thanks also to the authors of the hundreds of books I have read that empowered me to avoid the pitfalls and to enjoy the lessons they learned through their experiences, both good and bad. I have discovered that finishing the first draft is only a small step of many needed to complete the task of communicating knowledge and experience, and have come to appreciate the special role that authors have in enriching each of our lives.

Introduction

When we hear that 85% of the businesses that start fail within 3-5 years, we may shake our heads and think "That's a pretty high number." On paper, those are the hard numbers—the hard facts. What we often don't realize is that behind the facts are people like you and me—men and women who had a dream, who put their whole heart and soul into their business. They sacrificed their sleep, their personal and family life; they invested money, blood, sweat and tears to make "the American dream" their reality. Most of them had no idea what they were getting into. They were not equipped with the tools and techniques that would give them the power to succeed.

That is why I wrote this book: To share my years of experience and accumulated knowledge so that you will be equipped to succeed. During my business travels in South East Asia, I encountered a salutation that inspired the title of this book. Whether it was used as greeting or to sign off on an e-mail, the phrase "More Power!" conveyed the sentiment that I want to extend to you. It is a form of blessing, a desire for you to achieve more success and abundance in both your business and personal life.

When someone is a great chef, friends and family may tell him, "You should start a restaurant." He knows how to prepare delicious meals, but without marketing, sales, accounting, financing and management skills, chances are he won't be in business very long. Running a restaurant successfully requires more than knowing how to prepare good food. You can be a very skilled technician, yet to build your own business requires more power than just being good at your profession.

Business failure and business success both have a tremendous affect on your personal life. When the business runs the owner instead of the other way around, family life suffers, marriages break up, kids feel their parents don't care, etc. Some people are very resilient; others get burned out and give up on their dreams. They may have the potential, but are missing the key components and the basic facts. To achieve a fulfilled and balanced life, you need more than just the power of determination.

Do you remember the magazine advertisements that said "Build an oscilloscope", "Build a television", "Learn electronics at home"? Well, I was one of those geeks that bought all of those courses. I built an oscilloscope that operated with vacuum tubes, then one of the first solid-state oscilloscopes.

As a teenager, I was so interested in electronics that sometimes I would spend hours on a project for several days in a row. When I was done, I would turn on the power, full of expectations—nothing happened. That was so frustrating! After everything I put into it, it didn't work!

Sometimes business is like that. You've read the books, you've taken the classes, you've been to the seminars, but when you try to put it all together to see it work, nothing happens. Or worse yet, sparks fly and you trip a circuit breaker. So what do you do? Some might throw in the towel and decide to find another project. Not me; I would get out the instructions and start retracing and rechecking every step and every component to figure out what I did wrong.

As a serial entrepreneur, I apply the same strategy. Whenever something doesn't work out, I find out what went wrong and what I have to change to achieve the results I want. It hasn't been an easy journey, but I've learned a lot in the process. I discovered that businesses, like electronic devices, will not power up unless they are built correctly.

More Power! is more than just a set of instructions or a recipe for how to build your business. It will give you the understanding and comprehension of what a really successful business looks like and how you can achieve success with fewer struggles and less pain. My intention is to guide you and give you insight into the whys behind each step, so that when you finish creating your business, you can come up with an innovative marketing plan and take it to new heights. You can flip the switch, turn on the power, and see your creation become a reality.

Whether you are a new or accomplished entrepreneur, there will always be some adjustments that you will need to make. You are going to have some disappointments. You are on an exciting journey that may at times rush you to the top of the mountain, and subsequently take you through challenging valleys. You might round a bend to discover a beautiful sunrise or be suddenly confronted by rock slides blocking the road. I am your guide and I will give you advice on the best paths to take and warn you, in advance, which curves to look out for, as well as which roads have no guardrails.

I love the sport of business and as with any game, there are rules that can actually be used to your advantage, if you know them and apply them correctly. What you're about to discover is the most logical and powerful way to design and run your business, taking it from the theoretical to real life, measurable results. I urge you to take advantage of and benefit from the principles, strategies, and tactics you'll learn in this book. You could read a dozen books to glean the information that you will find packed into *More Power!*. Read carefully, but most importantly, implement the ideas that connect with you.

The difference between a manager and executive level leadership is the ability to make a decision and act on it, for better or for worse.

Grab your pen, a highlighter, and a notepad and get ready for action!

Bob Bare

CHAPTER ONE

Vision, Purpose and Destiny

I magine yourself stretching a rubber band between your hands. There's a tension created in the rubber band. You can allow that tension to pull your right hand to the left, or you can allow it to pull your left hand to the right. In the same way, you can choose to allow creative tension to pull your present reality closer to your vision. You can also choose to decrease the size of your vision to be closer to that of your present reality.

Have you ever turned down an opportunity to speak, or sing, or attempt to do something great, because you were afraid you weren't good enough? I see the same thing happen to people with great business ideas. To prevent this, it's very important to understand what vision is and to keep your focus on it.

The difference between your vision and your current reality is a source of energy. Get ready for some motivating discoveries that will take you to new levels if you implement what you're

1

about to learn. The first step on your journey is becoming aware of your vision.

In book after book the same questions are asked: What's your mission statement? What's your vision for your company? Or, what's your company's sales goal for this year? There are so many different definitions and so many misconceptions about what vision, goals, purpose, and destiny are that for some people, it all runs together.

Have you ever participated in a small group session of a workshop where you were asked to design a mission statement for your company? What comes out at the end is often something that's created to sound good to the public, to look good in a marketing campaign, or to be something that everyone agrees can be easily attained. Unfortunately, it usually is not the type of vision that can be used to unite your people and drive your company to a place it would never get without a written powerful vision.

Vision has to do with what you see in your mind as the ideal end result of your efforts. Vision is usually something very personal, which comes from within. There are two common mistakes people make which take power away from a well-defined vision.

The first mistake is to take a goal and mislabel it a vision. You might say, for example, "I want my company to operate with a 20% profit margin." What you've just stated is a goal, not a vision.

In moving you closer to your vision, we must first discuss purpose because a person's vision is hard to understand if analyzed separately. Purpose is this sense of *why* in your life—the reason that you are motivated to work hard to attain your vision.

To discover the purpose behind a goal, ask "Why?" If I were to ask you why you want to make a profit, you might say, "To keep my employees working." If I asked why again, you might say, "I want to leave a legacy to my children, a business that's prosperous and in good health, even during hard times." Now you have stated the motivating forces behind your ambitions. The long-term aspiration for the future that is the deepest driver of your actions is your purpose.

I started mowing lawns before I was a teenager. In the beginning, as soon as I got paid I would find a place to spend my money. After I got my driver's license, I would envision myself driving a nice car. That dream helped me focus and, of course, before long, I had my car. However purchasing a car was merely a goal, not a vision. If someone had asked me why I wanted to own a car, my answer would have revealed that my main purpose for purchasing a car was to gain increased independence. If I extended that purpose into the future, I could have written a long-term vision with an end result of becoming a fully independent adult.

A lot of people have negative goals—things they want to avoid. They might want to move out of the poor school district they live in, or they'd like to start their own business as a way of getting rid of some of the conflicts and problems they have at work. They mistake simple avoidance of the negative with fulfillment of a vision. Your vision needs to be a long-term commitment to a desired outcome or accomplishment.

The second mistake that you should avoid is placing your focus on the means to obtain your vision rather than focusing on the vision itself. Many people confuse the tactics for attaining their goals, which is just part of the journey, with the end result, which is the final attainment of their vision.

Your goals are a personal or corporate sense of how you're going to end up where you are headed. Your vision is the optimal end result that you have in mind. Your purpose is the why behind your goals and vision. And your destiny is something that sometimes comes along and surprises you and everyone else, when the outgrowth of your vision is grander and yields greater results than you could see ahead of time.

Develop and verbalize what your vision is by becoming more aware of yourself. Just for this exercise, ignore what your present reality seems to be. What are the skill sets that you really enjoy implementing? What are you passionate about? What do you dream about?

Free yourself up by setting aside some time to be alone. Go to the lake, find a quiet spot at the library, or just schedule some thinking time away from distractions. Then think about this question: If you woke up tomorrow morning, and all of your time and money constraints were gone, what would you most enjoy doing with your life? Your desires, the things that you're passionate about, will give you some indication of what types of activities would align well with your vision.

Writing your vision down is extremely important. You can refine it, you can expand on it, and you can change it as your understanding grows, but unless you have it written—and carry it with you—it will easily slip from your mind.

The motivation to drive you to realize that vision is related to what your purpose is. The key to understanding your purpose is to ask yourself "Why?" Why would I be happy if I achieved that vision? Why would my family be happy if we reached that vision? Why would my employees be happy to see that vision fulfilled?

> " It helps to know exactly
> whose attention you want to attract. "

Fuel your vision by centering on activities that are in alignment with it. It's worth the time to talk about what your vision, the end result, would be. Talk to those close to you and to your employees about what they see as your vision and your purpose.

A person who is fully aware of their vision (and the purpose underlying it) will attract other people who are motivated by the same desires. Your power, your energy, and your positive attitude will be a mystery to people who don't know the power of focused intentions.

When you're de-motivated, when you're down, when you've lost the enthusiasm and the zest that you had when you began a new project, it's time to get away and refocus on your vision and the purpose underlying it. This is when it becomes extremely helpful to be able to reach into your pocket or purse and pull out your written vision.

Close your eyes and visualize what you will feel like when you're at the place of fulfilling your vision. Imagine how your family will feel and imagine how happy your true friends will be when you have achieved the vision you decided to pursue. Without a written vision, your plans will perish. Once your vision is written down, you can keep it in front of you every day so that you can stay on course.

Don't make the mistake of developing a vision that is so easy to attain that you can do it in a short period of time, such as in one year. Make your vision bold. Make it so large that it almost seems impossible to attain. Then take a realistic look at where you are now. There will be a certain amount of creative tension between where you are now, and where you intend to be.

Don't be concerned about figuring out every step between where you are now and where you want to be. Later, we will talk about setting up milestones, goals, and actionable steps. Right now, realize that the creative tension between where you are now and where your vision says that you will be is a good thing. Choose to hold true to your vision, and don't allow yourself to become complacent.

George Bernard Shaw said this:

This is the true joy in life: Being used for a purpose recognized by yourself as a mighty one, being a force of nature instead of a feverish, selfish little clod of ailments and grievances, complaining that the world will not devote itself to making you happy.

—Shaw, Man and Superman, 1950

Achieving your vision requires more than creative tension. It also takes time. An acorn can lift a sidewalk, but it takes years. So take the steps necessary to attaining your vision. Set aside time to create your vision. Then write it down. Keep it with you and focus on it. The creative tension between your present reality and your vision will force your subconscious mind to provide you with ideas and solutions for how to move in the direction of your vision.

In the late 1980s I started a wholesale hearing aid repair business. I was the classic example of a technician who thought he would be happier running a company. I had spent several years in the corporate world, and decided I wanted to go back to being my own boss. Unfortunately, I made the mistake of getting too involved in the inner workings of the business, and painted myself into a corner.

I tried unsuccessfully for several years to sell the business through traditional means. One day after reading Robert Ringer's book called *Action: Nothing Happens Until Something Moves,* I decided to take action. I called up someone who'd shown an interest in the business a couple of years before and said "Look, I want to sell this business and I think you'd like to buy it. I'm buying an airplane ticket and coming to talk to you about it. Are you available any day this week, or should we make it for next week?"

That book helped me to create big changes in my life at a stage when I had reached a plateau. But before you take a bold action, you need to know where you want to end up. I think a great summary is, "Vision: Don't expect to arrive at your destiny unless you know where that might be."

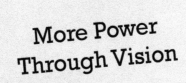
More Power
Through Vision

ACTION STEPS

1. Think about this question: If you woke up tomorrow morning, and all of your time and money constraints were gone, what would you most enjoy doing with your life?

2. Develop and verbalize your vision by becoming more aware of your major desires

3. Determine what your long-term vision is

4. Use the creative tension between where you are now and where your vision says that you will be to propel you in the direction of your vision

5. Recognize the motivating purpose behind your vision by asking yourself Why questions

6. Write out your vision and carry it with you constantly

7. Fuel your vision by centering on activities that are in alignment with it

CHAPTER TWO

Pre-venture Planning

Which do you feel more like, the tortoise or the hare? The classic story seems to imply that it's better to be slow and steady rather than fast and overconfident. I say you need both persistence and speed. You must have the ability to shift gears as your circumstances dictate.

There are times when it's important to be methodical, such as when you are compiling your research and due diligence. There are other times which require you to sprint. Change your mind set to fit the task at hand just as you would change gears to fit the terrain. There will be slow days when the persistence of the tortoise is required, but there will be many other days when you will need the speed of the hare.

We can't have more than 168 hours available to us per week, but we sure can accomplish a lot more within the time that we have. The first step in creating more time is to pay attention to the three Ds. With every activity on your to-do list, Discard it, Delegate it, or Do it. If you're not sure which category to put an item in, ask yourself these questions:

1. If I were to discard this, and not do it, how would that affect my life in the accomplishment of my vision?
2. Is there a reason why I need to be the person to do this, or could it be done almost as effectively by someone else?
3. If I am to do this, is it urgent, important, or both? Shall I do it now, or schedule it on my calendar?

> "Family needs to be one of your priorities. It's never a pleasing result when someone achieves their dream, their vision, only to discover that they are standing alone at the pinnacle of their success."

Your family, your church or your supportive social organizations, your friends, and your team all need to be included in your priorities and your time planning. Family needs to be one of your priorities. It's never a pleasing result when someone achieves their dream, their vision, only to discover that they are standing alone at the pinnacle of their success. One of the ways to clarify your priorities is to choose to spend time with those who are most important to you. When you visualize what it will be like to achieve your dreams, hopefully you can see your family there with you, your friends, and the team that has helped you get there.

I've found that avoiding the noon hour lunch rush by having an early or late lunch can add 30 to 60 minutes to my day. The time I spend driving to appointments becomes quality personal development time as I listen to self-improvement CDs and seminars. I admit that there are also times when I enjoy meditating, reflecting, or spending quiet time as I drive.

Even though I'm recommending being more efficient with your time, rest and relaxation are also very important. Entrepreneurs often go at a fast pace. It is important to take time to think and regroup. This is actually something that can be scheduled. Make sure part of your planning includes days off and time with friends and family.

I know that sounds impossible now, but first let's examine how much time most of us waste. Now, it may seem like a lot of work, but there is something to be said about taking an inventory of how you spend your time. Take a sheet of paper and list on one side the things that you currently do; on the other side, create a list of the things that you feel are important for you to do each week. You'll then be in a position to determine how to reschedule your life.

Waiting for service in restaurants, time you spend in the car, time spent watching television, and time spent checking up on Facebook friends and browsing through e-mails are all examples of areas that might be low-priority compared to what you really want to do with your time.

Without sounding harsh and unfeeling, I also want to point out that there are people who can be time wasters. Sometimes it becomes a disservice to your family, and to the attainment of your vision, to allow people to take more time than you would like on the telephone or in person. The ability to say no can be an important part of your arsenal in regaining control of your time.

One thing that I found very helpful is to set aside a period of time each day to accommodate chaos. You know it is going to happen! Why not schedule some time to do what didn't get done earlier.

Let's say you have time scheduled from 2:00 p.m. to 3:00 p.m. to make up for chaos. During the morning, your schedule was interrupted by an important customer. You spent an hour taking care of the situation. The task you had scheduled for that hour didn't get done. If it was urgent or important, you could move it over into that slot that you set aside for chaos management. Your task may not be accomplished at the time you schedule it, but at least you have some time set aside that gives you flexibility.

You've probably heard about the 80/20 rule, also known as the **Pareto Principle**: it states that for many events, roughly 80% of the effects come from 20% of the causes. Concentrate

your most productive hours, the times you have the most energy, on the 20% of your activities that are the most important to achieving your vision.

We've heard the cliché "Time is money." Well, if you don't have enough time, it wouldn't be surprising if you feel that you don't have enough money, either. Especially in a new business, money seems to be at a premium. It is possible to self-fund your growth. I managed to grow a company from $0 to $2.5 million in annual sales in less than four years, with no borrowed money. It sounds good, but it also creates its own set of problems. If you're a stock market investor, you know that often a parabolic stock chart precedes a sharp pullback and a period of consolidation, before the proof can be healthy again.

One of the strategies that others and I employ to grow new ventures with smaller capital requirements is the use of innovation, specifically, innovation in marketing. There are new ways to reach your target market without spending large sums on traditional advertising. We'll cover more about that in the chapter on marketing.

A second strategy that enables a quick start with a lower initial investment is the use of joint ventures and strategic partnerships. That will be covered more in chapter 9 when we talk about leverage.

The third strategy that allows you to self-fund the growth of a new enterprise is being willing to let it grow at a slower, more organic pace. That's hard for some personality types to do, but it can be a good choice.

Using OPM, or Other People's Money, can make things faster and easier, but there are definitely some downsides:

1. When you have larger amounts of money at your disposal, it's easier to spend money on things you really don't need. This makes your use of the money less efficient. And that's money that has to be paid back, either to the bank, private investors, or to your retirement savings. Have you ever watched children after they received an unexpected, large gift? It usually doesn't stay in their hands very long. And you've read stories about some of the financial disasters that happen when people who are not accustomed to large sums of money win the lottery.

2. When investors are involved, you can certainly expect to lose some control and decision-making ability. You'll also always have the feeling of someone looking over your shoulder.

3. With venture capitalists (VCs), it's not uncommon for them to require a controlling interest. They're looking for a magnificent return on their investment,

and only need to get that on a very small percentage of companies that they invest in. Founders of new ventures are sometimes shocked when their VC firm shuts them down, not because they are losing money, but because they're only mildly profitable.

4. During times of tight capital, business owners operating from a line of credit or credit cards can be put in a squeeze when their line of credit is cut off, or their terms are suddenly changed.

It's true that owning a small piece of a large enterprise is better than owning 100% of a business that doesn't make it. The mistake that many companies make is giving away too much of their business too soon. The more history you can create, the more "proof of concept" you can demonstrate, the more you can show a greater value for your business. The amount you can borrow, or the amount that investors will be willing to put into your company, will be increasingly larger as your company performs longer and more profitably.

That brings us to your plan. In my earlier years in business, I started, operated, and sold a number of businesses without having a written business or marketing plan. Having run businesses both with and without, I believe now those earlier businesses would have been much more successful if I had invested the time and energy into developing a worthwhile plan.

It's like going on a trip with some idea about where you're going, but with no detailed road map. You may eventually arrive at your destination, but it will usually take much more time and gasoline than if you had started with the road map.

Your business plan gives you a written document that will include how you plan to market your product or service.

We've already talked about the vision. The business plan is the blueprint for how to get you from your present reality to your vision.

Having a written business plan can prevent your business from failing. If you've ever created a business plan, you know it's not a simple thing to do. A lot of people create business plans as quickly as they can by filling in the blanks in a software program. That's not what I'm talking about when I say you need a written business plan.

The reason most people create a business plan is to obtain investors for their businesses. But in the process of researching its creation, you will discover many things that will help you establish a strong business and prevent problems. If you invest enough energy into it, developing a business plan will be one of the most important things you can do to create a lasting business.

The business plan basically answers questions. It answers questions that investors will have, questions that bankers have, and questions that you should have. Here are some of those questions:

1. Who are you, and why should I listen to you?
2. Where are you in your process of business creation?
3. Where are you going? What's your vision and purpose?
4. What's your product or service?
5. Who wants it?
6. Why would they want it?
7. How many people in which markets want it?
8. How are you going to tell them about it?
9. Who else has it, now?

10. How are you different from them?
11. What are the risks involved?
12. How much will it cost to get your products or services to those who want it?
13. What do you have to bring to the table?
14. What are the possible rewards?
15. What do you want (debt, equity investors, bond holders)?
16. What is your exit strategy? (When do I get my return?)

Those are all very important questions. In a traditional business plan, answering question number 11 about the risks involved is referred to as the SWOT analysis. The acronym stands for Strengths, Weaknesses, Opportunities, and Threats. If you honestly sit down with your team and enumerate each one of these four areas, you will have gone someplace and done something that many small business owners have never done. The fact that you've done this kind of analysis about your business will not only reassure your banker or investors, but it should be reassuring to you.

There are some very key things that an investor will be looking for in your business plan. If you have analyzed these critical components of a successful business and can present them to an investor, you can come out of the negotiation in a much stronger position. Here are the five areas in which you need to show a strong understanding:

1. Is there a pent up consumer demand?
2. Can you show that your product or service will be accepted well by the consumer?

3. What is the record of your management team, and are your managers strong enough to handle growth? If not, what additional team members will you need?

4. Do you have anything that is proprietary, and are there barriers to entering this field that will give you leverage over competition?

5. What's the risk/reward ratio? There's always risk. Does the opportunity for reward seem great enough to justify the risk?

After several months of toiling through the research and meetings necessary to answer all of those questions in a manner that will satisfy a battle-hardened banker or venture capitalist, you will know yourself and your opportunity much, much better than before you began. You'll also have a much greater chance of surviving tough times and unexpected challenges.

In between your present reality and your vision, you will need to create mileposts, which are major accomplishments along the way. Between those mileposts you will have intermediate goals. And you can reach those goals by breaking them down into actionable steps.

Commitment is a necessary ingredient for you to have staying power for long-term survival. One piece of ancient advice says that before you build the tower, you should count the cost. Creating your business plan and marketing plan is part of that process of counting the cost. It may seem like hard work, but it will have a tremendous payoff.

Plan For More Power

ACTION STEPS

1. Develop a business plan
2. Create a list comparing everything you currently do with the tasks that will help achieve your vision
3. Discard or Delegate the tasks that are not in alignment with your vision and focus on Doing all of the tasks that are
4. Schedule time to relax, think and regroup
5. Set aside a period of time each day for chaos
6. Perform a detailed SWOT analysis
7. In between your present reality and your vision, create mileposts

REMEMBER

- Developing a business plan will be one of the most important things you can do to create a lasting business.
- Make sure part of your planning includes days off and time with friends and family.\

CHAPTER THREE

Start-Up

A few months ago, some friends and I were eating lunch together at an after-church potluck. As my wife walked by the table, one of the men said to her, "Jan, Bob just came up with a great new business idea!"

My wife didn't even stop walking. She rolled her eyes, and said, "Not another one!"

Yes, she knows me well. As Loral Langemeire mentioned in the forward, I've started so many businesses since I was a teenager, I've lost track. Thankfully, they have become increasingly successful, as I've learned my lessons well, through failure, success, experience, reading, and great mentors. So many people are interested in working for themselves, especially in tough economic climates, that I'd like to share some thoughts on the critical keys to success for a new business.

If you search online for checklists on starting a new business, you'll come up with a lot of similar ideas. I'll list some of what you will find, and then give you what I've found to be more important, and even critical, if you want to have one of the few start-ups that stays around longer than five years. Here is a typical start-up checklist: (<u>Caution! DO NOT follow this list in this order, unless you *want* to fail</u>!)

- Select a name for your company
- File an assumed business name with your county or state
- Meet with an attorney, or create a business entity online, by incorporating or filing an LLC (Limited Liability Company)
- Order business cards
- Rent space or set up a home office
- Open a checking account
- Get telephone and Internet lines installed
- Set up relationships with professionals: a CPA, banker, attorney, business advisors
- Get licenses and permits in order
- Capitalize—set up lines of credit, borrow money, or look for investors
- Get insurance
- Set up record-keeping systems
- Set up financial systems with an accounting program
- Set your pricing
- Create a web page
- Write a business plan
- Write a marketing plan
- File for trademarks and patents
- Hire employees
- Send out a press release
- Start selling

NO, NO, NO again! This may be a typical start-up, but the typical startup fails! It is easy to be so in love with your product or idea, that you miss out on some of the very critical first steps. What if you go through all the steps above—which could take you a year or two—and discover, to your dismay, that there is not enough demand for what you are offering?

I once had a coworker I'll call Larry who had a brilliant idea for a specialized niche. I expected him to get right on it and begin selling it, but he would have none of that. There were bells and whistles to implement, trademarks and patents to consider. Then there were plans to add additional functions, to make his a multi-function miracle machine. Several years went by, and his idea started showing up in trade magazines, at trade shows, and in various applications. Unfortunately, none of the machines were Larry's. Someone else saw the opportunity, pounced on it, and created a great income from it.

I'm sure with enough time and money, Larry would have found or designed something that could be patented. He would have been better off just marketing it from the start. He had requests, the buyers were begging him for the equipment, but he just told them it wasn't available yet. It was sort of like a farmer having an apple tree full of ripe apples, and not picking them because he was working on building a machine to automate the picking.

There are several crucial issues that you can explore, inexpensively, before you invest heavily in an untested idea. Here are some suggestions:

1. **Is there demand for your product or service?**
   Forget focus groups. People have a tendency to say

what they think you want to hear, especially if they're getting paid for their advice. Instead, consider a Google AdWords Pay-Per-Click campaign. You can create sponsored ads promoting your idea or product. When someone is intrigued or interested by your headline, they will click on it, and find an interesting page that leads them to answer a survey to qualify for a free report, an excerpt, a sample, or to be put on a list to be notified when your product or service becomes available. You win by discovering how much traffic you can generate (try several different headlines and approaches). You may be able to start building an e-mail list of future customers who have opted in for future information, and you can get unbiased feedback and opinions. Since you aren't selling anything yet, the people who contact you won't feel threatened.

2. **If there is a market for what you are offering, are there gathering places where you can find potential customers?** It's easier to market to niche groups and loyal groups, which you can find in one spot. Are there discussion groups, organizations, or clubs that would be interested in your offer? Find their chat rooms, or their Facebook pages, or their common interest associations. Contact them. Join discussion groups and ask members for their opinions. People like to be asked for advice and if you aren't selling anything yet, you won't be spamming, and you may learn and gain great ideas. If your market is so dispersed you can't find a gathering place, it may be difficult to make contact when you are ready to roll.

3. **Does the market you are targeting spend money?** Don't expect college students to spend money on retirement annuities. Some groups are known buyers, such as golfers and Harley Davidson owners. Make sure you are targeting a group that willingly parts with their money, and that has money to part with!

4. **Go niche, if possible, rather than wide.** A target market that is well-defined will attract greater interest than a less well-defined market. People are interested in products and services that distinctly apply to them, rather than a "one size fits all" approach.

5. **Now is the time to do market research.** Define your ideal prospect precisely. Write a bio of your ideal customer, and write marketing geared to that person. Who is your competition, and what will you offer that they do not?

6. **Is this the right timing?** I remember a time about 25 years ago, when I owned a hearing aid repair company. I was constantly being asked if there were any courses available on how to repair hearing aids. Finally, I succumbed to the requests and created a course. It ended up being taught in multiple states, to classes of 10 to 25 hearing aid dispensers and audiologists, and was expanded to a video repair course. The timing was right.

A few years later, in the early 1990's, I decided to offer hearing aid repair directly to the consumer via the Internet.

Very few people took advantage of the offers, even though the rates were half of what a local hearing aid dispenser would charge. My target market generally did not have Internet access, and those that did wouldn't trust their credit card number being used on the web. The timing was wrong.

In 2006, I started virtually the same hearing aid repair offer on the Internet. It worked out to be a fantastic business, and is still generating new sales every month five years later. The target market had Internet access, and was comfortable doing business with my company via the Internet and email. The timing was right.

Ironically, I also tried offering my hearing aid repair seminars in the early 2000's, and received very little interest. The market had changed from mom and pop hearing aid stores to franchises and chains, and no one was interested in in-office repair.

The moral of the story is that you must prove your concept is marketable, including the timing. It is just as bad to be too early as it is late. There've been many businesses that were poorly run that made a lot of money for awhile. The timing was so good; almost anyone could succeed in that time period. (Think dot.com) The real test comes when times get tough. If your business can prosper and grow during tough economic times, you'll know you have learned some major business success principles.

7. **Your marketing plan is more important than your business plan.** Yes, I believe in writing a business plan. It makes you think through a lot of possibilities, such as your SWOT analysis. But a great business plan and great systems are wasted without a great marketing plan.

No matter whether you are for profit or non-profit, every concept is *selling* something. So start with selling. I'd rather see someone selling an idea or a prototype at a swap meet, or online with Google AdWords to test their concept, than writing a detailed business plan (although it is important, as we discussed in the last chapter) with no proof of concept! I have often been in the situation where I had orders flooding in, without perfected systems to handle them—and you do need to have both sales coming in and a great system to fulfill the orders. Personally I'd rather have the sales and be working on my system than have a perfect system and no sales!

This takes us to the subject of proof of concept, which is critical if you have plans to get investors involved. Ideas are wonderful, but we've all heard the cliché: "Ideas are a dime a dozen." Taking action on an idea, however, and creating a method to monetize it, is one of the first steps in creating proof of concept.

Until you've proven that people are willing to reach for their wallets and buy into your concept, you have a dream, not a business.

Put your ideas into writing, test them, measure the results, readjust your actions to improve the results, and modify your plan. Your written records are part of proving that your concept is valuable and marketable.

Competition is the next area on which you should focus your attention. Make two lists:

• What are all of the similarities between you and anyone with a similar offering?

- What are each of the differences between what you are offering and what other businesses have available?

These two lists become very important for the next step. That step is creating strategy for how you will be different from your competition.

Eliminate—What can you eliminate from what you offer that is unnecessary, unimportant to your customers, and will help you provide a lower price point or better service by not including it in your offer?

Reduce—In what ways can you reduce or lower what's included in your offer, compared to the competition?

Add to—What can you add to what you are offering that few or none of your competitors have?

Create—What new value can you create that no one else has?

By thinking through and implementing these steps, you can create something that sets you apart. Eliminate, reduce, and lower in areas that are traditionally offered but unimportant. Then add to and create added value products and services, and see how you stand out, like an eagle among crows.

Okay, that takes us to our next subject: marketing! To me, that is where the fun begins!

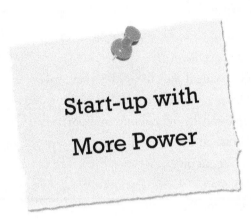

Start-up with More Power

ACTION STEPS

1. Do market research and answer the following questions
   a. Is there demand for your product or service?
   b. If there is a market for what you are offering, are there gathering places where you can find potential customers?
   c. Does the market you are targeting spend money?
   d. Is this the right timing?
2. Develop proof of concept by taking action on an idea, and creating a method to monetize it
3. Create a website in order to discover how much traffic you can generate
4. Put your ideas into writing, test them, measure the results, readjust your actions to improve the results, and modify your plan
5. Create a strategy for how you will be different from your competition

REMEMBER

- Your marketing plan is more important than your business plan.
- Go niche, if possible, rather than wide
- Eliminate, reduce, and lower in areas that are traditionally offered but unimportant
- Create added value products and services, and see how you stand out.
- No matter whether you are for profit or non-profit, every concept is *selling* something. So start with selling.

CHAPTER FOUR

Marketing

Marketing is a misunderstood subject. I'm going to help you understand marketing through a new lens—one you can relate to, especially if you've ever fallen in love.

Most people think of radio advertising, television commercials, the Internet, and print advertising when someone mentions marketing. These are the media that can be used to market your company. Most of the money spent on advertising is wasted, unless you understand what your *strategy* should be.

Marketing is simply building relationships between your company and individual consumers. You might object, by saying that relationships are only between people! Well, relationships are built between entities. Think of pets—you'd get slapped if you told someone they didn't have a real relationship with their beloved dog or cat! How do you build a lasting, loyal, passionate relationship between your customers and your company? Here are some of the keys.

First, your company must have an identity, a personality! Some people build the identity around themselves (think Steve Jobs), but I think it is easier to expand, duplicate, and especially to sell your business if the business has its own unique identity. There are a lot of books centered on this, usually focused on the word "branding," but I prefer the word identity, because it implies a personality.

Your company's identity, its personality, should not be phony! Look for your strengths and your unique benefits—focus on those. Here is a place to start: call some of your most loyal customers, or interview them in person, and find out why they buy from you. What makes them return to you, and not someone else? Hopefully, you offer more than just a low price, or you are in danger of becoming a commodity. What added value do you offer, or could you offer, that would give your business a personality trait that would endear you in your new relationships?

Being perceived as an expert in your field is a powerful force. How do you position yourself as an expert? Experts teach and provide information. Make sure educational materials, answers to questions, white papers, and reports are a prominent part of your offering.

What do you provide that your competitors do not? Give that uniqueness a personification. Remember the "You're in Good Hands with Allstate" commercials, where a person's hands had a house cupped in them? In literary terms, you want to use what your high school English teacher would call "anthropomorphism." That means giving human characteristics to something not human (your business). That's one concept from your English class that could make you a lot of money!

Answer this question: What can your business provide that would make your customers say, "I'd be crazy to buy from anyone else but you!"?

This concept of developing a personality, an identity for your business, is a good start. Spend some time on it. How can anyone build a loyal relationship to an impersonal business, with no emotions involved? Consider ways you could build some of the following emotions and emotion-based qualities into a relationship with your customers:

- Trust
- Loyalty
- Humor
- Joy
- Respect
- Excitement

Here is the second key towards developing a long-term relationship with your customers. *You need to be intensely interested in them*! Can you imagine going out on a date with someone, and all they ever did is talk about themselves? Yes, I know, some of you have experienced that. Isn't it much more interesting when someone wants to find out as much as they can about you?

This is called building rapport. How can you find common interests with someone and build rapport, without knowing something about them?

The best way that I can think of to begin this process is to create an ideal customer, sort of a compiled customer, so that you can envision who you are marketing to.

Let's say your primary market is women, in the 35 to 45 age bracket. What would be a precise, compiled customer? Write her profile. Let's say you decide a typical customer of yours might be Cassandra Williams, a 40-year-old receptionist, who works at a clerical job in a large corporation. She has three children, all in school. She loves jewelry and makeup, is a single mother, and spends a lot of time chatting with her friends on Facebook and by Instant Messenger. I could go on and develop the character more, but I'll stop here, to save time. I want you to get an idea of how to create a detailed profile.

If you fully develop your fictional, compiled customer, and write your marketing materials geared specifically to Cassandra—a person you keep in mind as you write—your materials would have much more clarity and focus!

Write down these things about "your" Cassandra:

- What are Cassandra's desires?
- What are her dreams?
- What are her goals?
- How can your offer improve the quality of Cassandra's life?
- How can your offer improve Cassandra's relationships?

What are your customers' core buying emotions? How can you present yourself so that your customers, instead of saying "I'm not interested," say "Tell me more, now!"

If you look at marketing in terms of building a relationship, everything starts to make sense. A lasting relationship develops in stages, such as:

a. Attention-getting stage (the eye contact stage)
b. Development stage (building rapport and common interests)
c. Romance (including education and trust building)
d. Power struggle (who is in control, applicable in some sales and closing situations)
e. Stability (keeping your customer)
f. Commitment (here is where referrals start)

Remember, it takes two to tango. Before you can ever get to that last stage, you need to start at the beginning, which involves getting your prospects' attention and starting communication—the start of the romance.

Secret desires are not really hidden to someone who's willing to listen. Listen carefully to what you hear your customers saying. Listen carefully to what's being said in social media such as Facebook, forums, and in chat rooms. If you can offer something that will fulfill those desires, then you have something that people will pursue rather than you having to chase them.

> " It helps to know exactly whose attention you want to attract. "

Many messages flood us all every day. From the e-mail, to social networking, to billboards and text messages, we are in an age of information overload. Stop your prospects with something that gets their attention, if you don't want to lose their interest.

It helps to know exactly whose attention you want to attract. Specific and powerful messages that are geared to a niche market are much more <u>effective</u> than a generalized message created to appeal to many.

Relevant information will get your customers' attention much more quickly. Internet research has shown time and again that people respond in greater numbers to relevant information. That insight is what made the founders of Google billionaires. If you learn to utilize it, you can increase your wealth, also.

When someone searches using a specific keyword phrase, it is proven that they are much more likely to click on a search result that also contains that exact keyword phrase. When they then land on a web page that contains again the exact keyword phrase somewhere at the top of the page, they will spend more time reading that page than if they did not immediately see the same words.

Once you've gotten someone's attention, you have to be able to keep their interest.

Internet marketers refer to the "bounce" rate of the page. It refers to the number of people that leave a website without ever going past the first page. There is nothing on that first page that is relevant or interesting enough to hold their attention, so they leave. The same thing happens in verbal communications. If you're speaking to a group of coworkers or just talking to a friend and you don't say something that is interesting to them, they may "leave the page" mentally, whether they appear to be listening to you or not.

So how can you add to the interest? One way is by arousing curiosity. Another way is by telling an interesting story.

Engaging your listener or your reader so that they feel like they are participating, even mentally, in your dialogue can keep them interested.

Romance in a relationship between two people continues to hold interest and attention. What is it about romance that fascinates us so much? Part of it is possibilities, imagination, and excitement. Good marketing introduces those aspects of romance to the relationship between business and customers.

Romance is such a critical aspect of the client/business relationship because it can create loyalty and commitment. Brand awareness is great, but brand loyalty is even better. Three aspects of developing a romantic relationship are time, good communications, and having common interests and affinities.

In an individual, one-on-one relationship between a business owner or his salesperson and a client, quite often a tension occurs. This tension is referred to by some as a power struggle. Which person has the most influence? Who is in control? Who will win? The easiest way to avoid that type of adversarial relationship is to make it clear from the outset that you as a business owner have the best interests of the client in mind. They must see your role as being on their side—as a consultant—and eventually, almost a friend.

One of the great values of developing a romance between your business and your customers and also taking a consultant/ sales approach, is that you are almost assured of repeat sales, referrals, and a long-time loyalty. The lifetime value of every client is often much greater than any single purchase.

More Marketing Power

ACTION STEPS

1. Develop your company's brand by focusing on your strengths and unique benefits
2. Position yourself as an expert by teaching and providing information
3. Answer this question: What can your business provide that would make your customers say, "I'd be crazy to buy from anyone else but you!"?
4. Build positive emotions into the relationship with your customers
5. Create an ideal customer so that you can envision who you are marketing to
6. Add to the interest of your marketing material by arousing curiosity or by telling an interesting story
7. Make it clear from the outset that you as a business owner have the best interests of the client in mind

REMEMBER

- Most of the money spent on advertising is wasted, unless you understand what your *strategy* should be.
- Marketing is simply building relationships between your company and individual consumers.
- Specific and powerful messages that are geared to a niche market are much more <u>effective</u> than a generalized message created to appeal to many.

CHAPTER FIVE

Team Building

F ailure is a frightening word to most people. In reality, every failure is a great learning opportunity. Some of my early mistakes during my first few start-ups would be a lot more costly if I were to make the same mistakes now with a much larger company. Let me tell you about a concept that I've learned that has made my life much easier, and my businesses much more successful.

One of the biggest mistakes I've ever made, and it's a very common reason for business failure, is to think that I have all the skill sets necessary to run a business. There are three major aptitudes that are required for every successful business, and very few people have all three of them. A successful business does need a visionary, someone with leadership skills who sees the big picture and is willing to take risks. Also needed is someone that has great sales and marketing abilities. The final piece is someone that has strong financial and administration skills. The three actually tend to be mutually exclusive. How many super salesmen have you met that were also strong in administration?

Which of those three do you think is your predominant strength? Do you have a deep understanding of financial management, and the ability to analyze key performance indicators? If that's you, it is likely that you would do well to have someone else that's strong in sales and marketing. Here's what you can do if you're weak in one or two of those three areas: You can hire someone that's highly skilled in your weaker areas, or you can bring in a partner, or even outsource that part of your business.

> " Leadership and vision, sales and marketing, and administration and finance are like three legs of a stool. "

If you fill these three basic needs well from the beginning, your business will be off to a much more powerful start. Leadership and vision, sales and marketing, and administration and finance are like three legs of a stool. Without any one of the legs, the stool will be unstable and topple. Start your team by filling these three areas with powerhouses, because they'll provide a stable base—a strong foundation.

After the base that's needed on the executive team, there are ten aptitudes that either you, someone else on your team or your combined team must possess. They are:

1. Initiative
2. Planning

3. Innovation
4. Ability to handle change
5. Sales skills
6. Negotiating skills
7. Communications
8. People management
9. Faith and/or persistence
10. Team-building talent

Like a well-balanced personality, the team requires time and effort to develop. A great book to give you a better understanding of how to go about that is, *The Five Dysfunctions of a Team*, by Patrick Lencioni (Jossey-Bass; 1st ed., April 11, 2002).

There are two different management styles that most people are familiar with. One is the traditional, top-down, organizational chart management that predominated during the 20th century. The other is team-centered and holistic, functioning more like an organism. There is actually a place for both.

My personal preference is for everyone to operate and cooperate as a team, treating each other with equality and respect. I guess I'm an idealist. I've also learned a lot of people can't function well without an organizational chart to guide them as they learn how to operate as a team member.

Begin with an organizational chart, so that everyone has clarity on where they fit in, how authority is distributed in the organization, and what parts of their job they have autonomy in. With that perspective, you can train your people to work and cooperate as a team.

Too many people hire their team members based on their education and their résumé. What is strikingly overlooked is how each team member's personality and temperament blend with the part of the team you are asking them to join.

Most people are very familiar with one or more personality tests. These tests typically divide people into four major categories. The four groups are given names like director or commander, analyst, people person or enthusiast, and amiable or calm. Rather than trying to match résumés with job descriptions, I've had great success with deciding before my first interview what personality type I want for a particular position. For example, in hiring a new receptionist, I knew in advance that I wanted a very personable, relational, social person for the job. I had applicants with amazing skills and education, who did not fit the personality profile I was looking for. Knowing in advance the personality that fit the job helped immensely in deciding on the best person.

Should you ask applicants to fill out a personality test? Absolutely! You might even use it as an online screening process that would help cut down on the number of interviews you have to do.

What about your present employees? Why not reevaluate them? Bring in someone who's trained in giving personality tests and team building. Someone who is a good employee can become a fantastic, productive person when they are in a position that is compatible with their personality and temperament.

After screening for types and personality, you should explain and discuss your company values and culture during the interview. In this way, there will be no surprises. For example, when I am interviewing to fill a position on one of our management teams, I tell people that I have some non-negotiable expectations, including that each member will exhibit trust and respect in relationship to other team members, and that I value freedom of expression in meetings, but want the team to remain cohesive.

What does an effective team meeting look like? The words that exemplify a great group of employees to me are passionate, expressive, non-judgmental, and respectful.

Another way to build a cohesive team is by having each manager train someone downstream to perform their job functions. I teach my managers that they cannot move upward unless there is someone they have trained to move into their position. Rather than being indispensable, I would rather have them training others to be able to do what they are good at. That way they become indispensable to the forward growth of the team, and can move up more rapidly because they have duplicated themselves in their former positions.

It is also valuable to cross-train team members, so that each person has the ability to take a vacation, without coming back to a mountain of work. As more people learn each job, they can collaborate, and create new systems and ideas.

Financial incentives are greatly overrated. Many people will stay longer at a job they love, with team workers they value, when they are incentivized in other ways. Daniel Pink, in the book *Drive*, mentions three forms of incentives much more powerful than money. Those three drivers are:

1. Autonomy (not having to be micromanaged, but having some self-directed aspects)
2. Mastery (send your team members to workshops and trainings to become great)
3. Purpose (find what your team members value, and let what they are doing contribute to what they find value and fulfillment in)

Not only can developing a great team be rewarding financially and emotionally, you'll soon find yourself with time for other pursuits when your team begins to buy in and take ownership of your vision and values.

Build A More Powerful Team

ACTION STEPS

1. Make sure your executive team has members who fulfill the three primary aptitudes areas:
    a. Visionary leadership
    b. Sales and Marketing
    c. Financial and administration
2. Determine which aptitude is your predominant strength
3. Build the rest of your team so that you cover the ten secondary aptitudes
4. Begin with an organizational chart, so that everyone has clarity on where they fit in
5. Bring in someone who's trained in giving personality tests and team building
6. Have each manager train someone downstream to perform their job functions

7. Motivate your team with the three forms of incentives that are much more powerful than money. Those three drivers are: autonomy, mastery, and purpose

REMEMBER

- There are three major aptitudes that are required for every successful business, and very few people have all three of them.
- Leadership and vision, sales and marketing, and administration and finance are like three legs of a stool. Without any one of the legs, the stool will be unstable and topple.
- Knowing in advance the personality that fits the job will help immensely in deciding on the best person for that position.
- Like a well-balanced personality, the team requires time and effort to develop.

CHAPTER SIX

Culture

Google is known for their company culture.

- Café stations where employees can chat and enjoy free food
- Game rooms, with video games and foosball, for breaks at any time
- Bicycles stationed outside of each building's front door to grab and ride to another part of the campus
- A baby grand piano, for playing and relaxation

Google created their company culture intentionally. You have a choice, to either intentionally decide and create your company culture, or let one develop by accident at the whim of your team. Choosing and nurturing your company's culture is the smart choice.

Company culture can make your workplace productive and enjoyable, or chaotic and discouraging. It will determine not only the level of productivity, but the results that are created, including profitability and employee retention. Creative, talented, and amazing people will want to come to work at a place where the atmosphere is positive and alive. And they will be willing to work harder and stay longer in a creative, enjoyable atmosphere.

> "Determine the values your company deem important, then make them a part of daily life."

Do the following descriptions sound like the type of workplace you would like to create?

- Positive
- Inspiring
- Creative
- Joyful
- Energetic

The way to achieve that type of environment is by deliberately choosing what you want your culture to be like, and then going about planning, creating, and nurturing it.

The beginning of creating an outstanding company culture starts with determining the values your company deems important, then making them a part of daily life. The values, and therefore the culture of a company, should come directly from the founder and leadership of a company, and be deliberately chosen and implemented.

A great garden doesn't just happen unexpectedly in your backyard. Specific steps have to be taken, including preparation of the earth, planning, planting, watering, and weeding. Most company cultures are like a backyard that is overgrown with weeds; it's just the mess that happens when no planning or care has been taken.

Here are some steps to begin the creation of a great company culture:

1. Set aside a time to get away, either by yourself, or with a few key people. Discuss and create a list of what your personal values and beliefs are. Eliminate the unimportant and reduce the list to between three and five key values.
2. Write a concise description of what your key values are, and which ones are non-negotiable.
3. Have copies printed and distributed at a dedicated company values meeting.
4. Teach yourself and your team to evaluate every decision based on whether or not the final choice fits the values that have been deliberately chosen as important.

During the Great Depression, Herbert J. Taylor was asked to take over and turn around a company on the brink of failure. The company owed $400,000 more than its assets, and was on its way down. Mr. Taylor accepted the challenge, even putting in his own money to keep the company afloat. Rather than concentrating solely on financials, Mr. Taylor chose to intentionally operate using a set of values to guide the ailing company, which was Club Aluminum.

After praying for guidance, he sat down to write some ethical guidelines for the company. His first statement was around 100 words, which he decided was too long. So he narrowed that to a list of seven bullet points, and then reduced it to only four questions to use as a litmus test about any decisions. Finally, he checked with his four department heads to get their take on his guidelines.

They included a Roman Catholic, a Christian Scientist, an Orthodox Jew, and a Presbyterian. They all agreed that the questions matched both their personal and their spiritual beliefs, and would provide an excellent guideline for the company.

The result was, "The Four-Way Test of the Things We Think, Say or Do," memorized by probably hundreds of thousands of Rotarians.

- Is it the truth?
- Is it fair to all concerned?
- Will it build good will and better friendships?
- Will it be beneficial to all concerned?

Simple and yet powerful, these four questions became the litmus test of any decision he or his managers made at the company.

The test sounds idealistic and impractical to many businessmen, but it worked for Club Aluminum. It created loyalty and goodwill with their customers, and proved to be a turning point in the fortunes of the company. By 1937, Club Aluminum's debts were paid, and during the next fifteen years, they distributed more than one million dollars in dividends to their stockholders. The net worth grew to more than two million dollars.

An accident? Luck? No, accidents happen to the careless and those who don't plan. By intentionally choosing, implementing, and maintaining values that are in line with the leadership of a company, a business will grow stronger, and a sustainable and useful culture will become established.

Here is another way to distill and clarify what your values and your company values are. Think about the ideal employee. What would the most perfect employee you can imagine be like? How would he or she treat clients, coworkers, and superiors? If you create the ideal in your imagination, then write down the details of what that perfect person would exemplify, you will have another way to determine the values you and your company should develop.

The reason that you want to have a clearly defined and developed company culture is the same reason that you would want a rudder on a ship, or a steering wheel on a car. Without the leadership of your company determining its culture, there is no control mechanism to guide and steer your company to your intended destination. You can express and instill the values and culture that you decide upon by using examples, stories, and by acting out and living the values that you want in your company.

Here are some examples of powerful cultural values that can change how a company operates:

- Service above self
- People before profit
- Honor commitment even when it costs
- Our people are our greatest asset

To summarize, here are two steps to identifying and developing a company culture:clarify your values, and then

<u>make your words and actions congruent with those values.</u>
The culture that is based on values can create unity and
teamwork among employees. You can also create customer
loyalty and referrals. To really create the winning team, you also
need to empower them with motivation.

The Power of Culture

ACTION STEPS

1. Intentionally decide on and create your company culture
2. Write a concise description of what your key values are, and which ones are non-negotiable
3. Clarify your values, then make your words and actions congruent with those values
4. Teach yourself and your team to evaluate every decision based on whether or not the final choice fits the values that have been chosen as important
5. Create the ideal employee in your imagination, then write down the details

REMEMBER

- The way to achieve a positive, productive environment is by deliberately choosing what you want your company culture to be like, and then going about planning, creating, and nurturing it.

- By intentionally choosing, implementing, and maintaining values that are in line with the leadership of a company, a business will grow stronger, and a sustainable and useful culture will become established.

Motivate

Motivating people is a skill that some people seem to come by naturally: some speakers are talented at it, but a lot of others have no idea where to start. Those individuals who do a great job motivating others, often aren't able to explain how they do it.

Psychologist Jonathan Haidt has an interesting theory that he calls the happiness hypothesis. He says that each person has two separate areas that must be addressed to get them motivated. Imagine a rider holding onto reins, but instead of riding a horse, he is riding an elephant. Dr. Haidt compares the elephant to the person's emotional side, and the rider to the same person's rational side.

The rider has a lot of influence as long as the elephant doesn't have any strong emotions. But if the elephant experiences high levels of anger, fear, sadness, or other strong emotional states, the rider loses control and the elephant is in charge.

So when we want to motivate someone, we have to understand and address their emotional state as well as their

rational side. Think of these as power emotions—driving emotions. As in sales and advertising, we need to be aware of the current emotional state the person is in if we want to inspire a different state.

The same principles of motivation apply to both your team members and your customers. I don't know who originated the phrase, but the best description I've heard for effectively communicating is to "enter the conversation in their mind." In other words, if you can figure out what people are thinking about, then you can seamlessly begin communicating with them as if you'd been reading their minds. You've just made a long stride towards success.

Hope is a powerful emotion. What does the person you're trying to reach hope will come true? Passion is another powerful emotion. What are the people that you would like to reach passionate about? Vision is related to hope. What if you can write a description that tells a story about your customer, and how it would feel to be living their vision?

One very powerful form of therapy is called *solution-focused brief therapy*. It focuses on what clients want to achieve through their therapy. Therapists use a question they call *the magic question*. Here is an example of the magic question taken from *Wikipedia*:

> Suppose our meeting is over, you go home, do whatever you planned to do for the rest of the day. And then, sometime in the evening, you get tired and go to sleep. And in the middle of the night, when you are fast asleep, a miracle happens and all the problems that brought you here today are solved just like that. But since the miracle happened overnight nobody is telling you that the miracle happened. When you wake up the next morning, how are you going to start discovering that the miracle happened? ... What else are you going to notice? What else?

If you can discover the answer to the magic question that your customer has in their mind, and describe to them in your ad or on your website how they will feel when their problem is solved, you will go a long way towards addressing the emotions that will cause your client to take action.

All this seems like such a tall order. Here's a way to make it easier. It's called small wins, or sometimes it's called baby steps. Instead of trying to persuade your potential customer to take a large step to get them where you want them to end up, motivate them to take small steps in the right direction.

If a member of your target audience sees a banner ad or a pay-per-click ad on the Internet, it should only address the emotions needed to get them to click through. When they reach your landing page, your headline should give them the motivation they need to read the first paragraph. Their interest should be piqued enough by the first paragraph to either continue reading or skip to the end to see what the price is. Don't try to accomplish everything at the same time. Each step should be geared only lead them to take the next step.

Here's an important second part to all of this. Books have been written about addressing the emotions. Selling has been defined as an emotion-based experience. However, as psychologist Jonathan Haidt so aptly points out, there is also a rider directing and trying to control the elephant, or the emotional side. You must, at the same time, address both the rational and the emotional parts of the brain.

Here are some ways to more effectively address the rational part:

- Clarity is very important. Spell it out
- Provide step-by-step instructions, so that no doubt is left about what to do next
- The enemy of the above two steps is ambiguity. Make it simple
- Help keep the focus on the destination by use of reminders and reiteration.

So far, I've been communicating with you about motivating customers. Everything above also applies to motivating your employees, your suppliers, and any person you come into contact with. You must address and consider both their emotions and their intellect.

With employees, especially, you need to reinforce their positive actions verbally and publicly. If you have negative actions that you have to correct, that should be done privately. For more details on this subject, a great book is, *Switch: How to Change Things When Change is Hard*, by Chip and Dan Heath (Broadway Business, 2010).

Motivate
With Power

ACTION STEPS

1. Learn to be aware of the current emotional state of the person you are dealing with

2. Discover what your target audience hopes will come true

3. Determine what your target audience is passionate about

4. Discover the answer for the magic question that your customer has in their mind

5. Write your sales copy in a way that addresses both the rational and the emotional parts of the brain.

6. Provide step-by-step instructions, so that no doubt is left in the minds of your target audience about what to do next.

REMEMBER

- When you want to motivate someone, you have to understand and address their emotional state as well as their rational side.
- Instead of trying to persuade your potential customer to take a large step to get them where you want them to end up, motivate them to take small steps in the right direction.
- The same principles of motivation apply to your customers, your team members, your suppliers, and any other person you come into contact with.

CHAPTER EIGHT

Metrics

I n the book, *The Art of War*, Sun Tzu makes a statement
critical to business owners. Many people know the
importance he places on *Full knowledge of one's enemies'
strengths and weaknesses,* but even more important is, as he
says, you must have *Full knowledge of one's own strengths and
weaknesses.*

Very few business owners, especially in small business, are
fully aware of their SWOT, as stated in a complete business plan.
Again, SWOT stands for strengths, weaknesses, opportunities,
and threats.

The way to be fully aware and be able to fine tune your
performance is by the use of metrics, a term more well known in
corporate America than in small business and entrepreneurship.
Metrics, of course, refers to measurements. The key, though, is
what you are measuring, and how you use that information to
keep your business sharp and on the cutting edge.

I'm not talking about looking at your income statement or
your balance sheet. Those are the typical instruments that most

people use to measure their performance, but their use could be compared to driving a car while looking in the rearview mirror. By the time you discover there's a stalled car in front of you, it may be too late.

A mentor and business advisor, Rich Allen, compares operating a business with no forward-looking metrics to flying an airplane at night in the clouds with no instruments. How do you know if the ground is getting closer, or if a mountain is 1,000 feet ahead?

Here are the types of metrics that will save your business from the side of a mountain. Use measurements of activities that must be done before business can take place. Let's look at some examples:

1. **Do you know your sales process?** How many steps are there in it? For example, here are some of the processes in one of my businesses:

a. Networking—collect leads of authors and potential authors

b. Learn their specific needs, desires, and vision for their project

c. Ask for contact information and permission to have one of our Book Writing Coaches/Consultants contact them to discuss future projects

d. Forward contact information to consulting department

e. Consultant contacts potential client to assess needs and ways we can assist them in writing, publishing, or marketing their book(s)

f. Ask potential client if they would like to receive any of the free educational or training guides that are available.

g. Original person who made referral follows up to make sure contact was made and helps with any questions

h. Follow-up sequence between consultant and author continues if there is continuing interest by potential client

i. Letter of intent, if appropriate, is sent

j. Blazon Press management discusses and decides if the book meets our guidelines or could be improved to a point where it would be marketable

k. Management team discusses and decides whether there is sufficient need or interest in the market for a book of this particular genre

l. If both of the above are met, an offer to publish is made to the author

m. Author coaching agreement, publishing agreement, and/or marketing plan is agreed to and formalized

2. **Measure and record numbers associated with each step in the process**

a. Continuing the publishing example, how many contacts are made each day and each week with potential clients?

b. How many of those potential clients gave their contact information?

c. How many were forwarded to the coaching/consulting department?

d. How many were contacted by a coach or consultant?

e. How many follow-up contacts were made by the original networker?

f. How many letters of intent were sent?

g. How many agreements were signed and for what dollar amount?

The activities you track should be measurable, repeatable, and improvable. What activities determine how many sales your business makes? Is it determined by the number of telephone calls someone makes, the number of clicks on a PPC ad on the Internet, or the number of visitors to your website?

3. **Arrange for daily or weekly reports to be sent**

Depending on how closely involved you are in overseeing the business, you want to know either daily or weekly what your "forward-looking numbers" are. In

the example above, let's assume the following numbers are average:

a. Contacts made: 12
b. Contact information received: 10
c. Contacts forwarded: 10
d. Coaching contacts made: 8
e. Follow-up contacts made: 8
f. Number of follow-ups per author: 3
g. Letters of intent sent: 4
h. Number/amount of signed agreements: 3

On your metric reports, you will begin to see averages and patterns. If the above numbers remained consistent over a number of months, you could begin to assume that for every twelve good networking contacts, you would end up with 3 signed agreements. If you know the "lifetime value of a client" to your company, you can determine the average value of each call you make. Then, finding a way to double the number of contacts in step a) would potentially double your sales in step h).

Here is where the beauty of metrics comes in. If you were able to double the number of contacts in step a) to 24, and the amount of sales remained the same, you would want to know where the problem was. You might be able to take a look at the other measurements and find out what went wrong. For example, if you saw d) was 16, but e) was 4, you would deduce that the person who met the potential clients was not doing their follow-up calls to answer questions and concerns, and this was causing the drop in completed contracts.

Another extreme benefit of having your regular metrics reports from the field is to be able to be proactive and prevent problems *before* they occur! If it normally takes thirteen weeks from step a) to step h) of the sales process above, you can tell up to thirteen weeks ahead of time if you will be having a problem in sales. If you only use your income statement to gauge your business, you may discover your revenue has fallen by a third or more at the end of a quarter. You sure don't want to wait for thirteen weeks to get your business back up—you may no longer be around by then!

If all this seems way too overwhelming to you, ease your way into it. You may have a hard time getting everyone at every step of your sales process to acquire the habit of sending in their reports, so break them in slowly. Here are some steps:

- Write down each step of your sales process. You can't track them unless you know what steps are available to quantify.
- Select one to three of the most critical steps to track, at first; not all of them. In the example above, I would say a), d), and h) would be the important steps to track (number of initial contacts, coaching contacts, and signed agreements).
- You may have to fight to get people to report their numbers. It makes them more accountable, and it takes time, so there will be resistance. In one business I know of, the CEO required the sales team to turn in their reports before they received their commission checks. I don't know the legalities of that, but it did work for him.

Until now, I've only been talking about designing metrics for your sales team. But you need to do this in all aspects of your business. After sales, comes production and fulfillment. If you have your sales perfected, but there are bottlenecks in fulfillment, the backlog will eventually become very bad news, and will start to affect your sales. If for no other reason, potential clients will hear about your slow turnaround time and fulfillment, and will choose someone else to do business with!

In the production and fulfillment part of your business, a good metrics system will show you where your chokepoints are, where there are pile-ups of work to be done, and allow you to find ways to release those points to get your team and production moving again.

You should be receiving reports from:

- Sales and marketing—predictive metrics
- Production and or fulfillment—tracking metrics
- Customer satisfaction—quality assurance metrics

Think of the dashboard of your car. At a glance you can see your speed, how much fuel you have, the engine temperature, and any early warning signs. In newer cars you can even check your miles per gallon and your tire pressure. With GPS, you can see the number of miles left to your destination. There are a lot of people driving their business with no idea how much fuel is left in the gas tank, and without knowing if they are still on track to their destination.

Once you begin getting raw data on a regular basis, you can start putting the numbers onto a chart, and you will begin to see trends before they reach critical mass. Once your metrics are in graphical form, your team will realize what is happening in the company, whether for good or bad. They can be motivated more easily with incentives, bonuses, or recognition, as mileposts are achieved.

Metrics not only creates accountability, but they provide clarity as to what is expected, and when recognition and awards will come. Even though they don't sound exciting in the beginning, when results are measured and success can be quantified, metrics can create rejoicing and rewards for the entire team.

The key steps to success with metrics are:

- Collect data (through the windshield, not the rearview mirror)
- Discern patterns
- Respond with changes and improvements (correct course)

Without this type of data, too many people confuse action and busyness with productivity. With metrics, it will become clear to your team which activities you are measuring and which tasks it is critical to focus on. Perfecting the art of metrics brings you closer to being a business ninja in the *Art of* (business) *War*.

Measure
Your Power

ACTION STEPS

1. Determine and describe every step in your sales/marketing, production/fulfillment, and customer satisfaction processes

2. Measure and record numbers associated with each step in each of the processes

3. Arrange for daily or weekly reports to be sent to you for analysis

4. Use the raw data to create charts, so that you can see trends before they reach critical mass

5. Respond to the trends that you discover with changes and improvements

REMEMBER

• The best way to become fully aware of your SWOT and be able to fine tune your performance is through the proper use of metrics.

- Without metrics, too many people confuse action and busyness with productivity.
- Once your metrics are in graphical form, your team will realize what is happening in the company, whether for good or bad.

CHAPTER NINE

Leverage

Wait! Don't even go there! Most people, as soon as they hear the word leverage, think about Donald Trump, real estate, and *Nothing Down* real estate investing. They automatically think of leverage as a debt ratio, having to do only with money. That is not what this chapter is about. This is about leverage as a business tool, not necessarily having anything to do with money.

The concept of leverage is ancient, going all the way back to Archimedes who said, "*Give me a place to stand, and I shall move the earth with a lever.*" As an entrepreneur, you can multiply your successes by discovering the principle of leverage.

When you use leverage, small changes can produce big results. The possibilities are endless, but you must have some understanding of leverage and what to look for. If you like the idea of turning $100 into $1,000,000, then pay attention to this lesson.

Leverage can be created by the use of three items: a fulcrum, a load, and an applied force. Here is a typical diagram illustrating the common understanding of leverage:

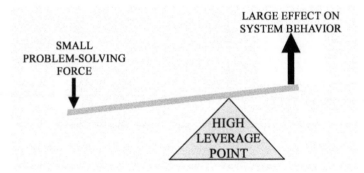

What most people don't think about is all the variations of leverage, and their applications. For example, here are three classes of leverage:

- Class 1: The fulcrum is located between the applied force and the load. For example, a crowbar, or a pair of scissors, or a seesaw.
- Class 2: The load is situated between the fulcrum and the force. For example, a wheelbarrow or a nutcracker.
- Class 3: The force is applied between the fulcrum and the load. For example, a pair of tweezers or the human mandible.

I can hear some of you saying "Get to the point—how does this apply to me?" I'll start with a real example, and then analyze it.

In 2006, I started a new business—a hearing aid repair lab—to leverage the power of the Internet and create an Internet-based hearing aid repair business. HearingHaven.com has developed into a fine business, but another revenue stream was created, quite by accident.

In the process of selling a previous business, I had to personally become certified as a qualified provider of hearing aids to a third party payer, in order for the buyer, then an employee, to be certified himself as soon as he became the owner.

After the sale, as the first year in my new business evolved, I realized I still held that certification, and wondered how clients could discover us. I wondered if there was a provider list. If someone Googled "Texas **** Hearing Aid Providers," would they find a list that had my company's contact information on it?

I did the search, and found ... nothing! There was no readily available provider list. Not only that, it was very difficult to locate any information about how someone who had this particular insurance in Texas could determine if they were eligible for hearing testing and assistance. A quick check of searches done the previous month showed there were indeed people searching for an answer, but without finding any usable results.

At that point, we did something that soon launched Hearing Haven.com into one of the fastest growing audiology clinics in Texas. I wanted to be found, and I had been taught an important lesson by one of my Internet marketing mentors, Ken McCarthy. He said that one of the best ways to connect with clients and establish your business as an authority was to provide free educational information.

We created an informational web page that laid out the steps and forms needed to get a provider to pay for a hearing aid in Texas. All the rules were laid out. For example, a physician had to do an exam and establish that there was no medical contraindication to hearing aids for that patient. We included a link to download a copy of the form needed at the next doctor's visit.

One of the last steps was to contact a hearing aid provider or audiologist who was already set up to be a provider under the appropriate rules in Texas. The web page closed by saying "To request the name of a qualified provider, please call one of the following toll free numbers" and there was a list of 800 numbers for different metropolitan areas and segments of Texas. Each of the numbers was forwarded to our main office (at that time our only office) in Texas.

Of course, the web page was optimized to be search engine friendly with proper SEO (search engine optimization), and a search engine pay-per-click (PPC) campaign was set up with the major search engines. Because the keyword phrases we were targeting were not common, within a week or two we were ranking in the top two positions of Google and Yahoo, and of course showing up across the Internet through the PPC campaigns. The calls started coming almost immediately, and our growth was launched.

It took almost three years before the competition caught on, and by that time we had established contracts, clinics, and long-term business relationships. We launched our successful business by leveraging the fact that there was no one else offering the information we supplied.

Let me repeat a sentence from the beginning of this chapter: "Leverage can be created by the use of three items: a fulcrum, a load, and an applied force."

How could the story above be described? I would say:

a. The *load* was the new business I wanted to create
b. The *fulcrum* was my existing business, HearingHaven.com
c. The applied force, the *lever*, was the web page and the SEO that made it high-ranking when using the search engines

It is not usually difficult to determine what load you want to move. It might be additional sales, or buckets of new leads, or multiplying the sales of a book. You might be looking for a copious amount of telephone inquiries, or wanting to multiply the number of donations your organization receives. Write down here or on a sheet of paper your response to the following:

What is the load or result you or your business wants to move?

Which business or part of your business is the fulcrum that you plan to rest your lever on?

Now the important part: What can you create, innovate, or use as the lever that will move your load quickly and easily?

Here are some ideas for a lever. I'll develop and expand on a few of them.

- Websites (discussed above)
- Joint ventures (developed below)
- Your customer list (example: sell another product line to them)
- Your sales force, if highly functional (market other's businesses, products, and/or services through them)
- Another businesses' sales force (market your products/ services through them)
- Your credit score, if good, someone else's credit score, if not
- Your established credibility, someone else's credibility
- Marketing techniques from <u>outside</u> of your industry
- Referral systems from <u>outside</u> of your industry
- Leads that you don't close, leads that your competitor doesn't close
- Sales to others of inquiries for a product/service you can't provide
- Inquiries that another business cannot use, that they will give to you
- Permission granted to another business to use your distribution system
- Use of another businesses' distribution system
- Marketing of your product/service through complementary businesses
- Permission given to complementary businesses to market themselves to your clients
- Use of your market positioning to attract leads for others

- Authoring a book (both for credibility and as a marketing device)
- Use of other businesses' marketing positioning to provide leads to you

Okay, let me get back to practical examples for some of the above ideas, to get you thinking. A story is told from the early 1900s, some saying it was initiated by one of the Rothchilds, others saying it came from Rockefeller or Buruch. Whichever wealthy icon it was, the story goes that a young entrepreneur approached the well-known, fabulously wealthy individual asking for a loan to finance a business. The wealthy business baron, knowing the value of leverage by association, told the entrepreneur:

"I'll walk across the floor of the stock exchange and back, arm in arm with you. Then you'll be able to borrow all the money you want."

Here is an example of the use of joint venture partners. When I started receiving telephone calls requesting the name of a third-party hearing aid provider in areas of Texas that were not practical for me to send someone to, I would do the following:

First, I would call hearing aid dispensers and audiologists near the town the client was in, and ask if they worked with this particular provider. At that time, most did not. If someone said yes, they already worked with clients of this payment provider, I would politely ask how that was going for them, and discuss what they had learned and share questions and observations with them. I would then say goodbye without telling them about the nearby prospect.

I would continue to make calls until I found someone who did not work with these clients, usually because of the hoops they needed to jump through to become certified and the medical billing expertise required. This gave me an opening to offer them the opportunity of contracting with our company in a partnership, with us providing the certification and billing submission expertise they needed, in exchange for time and services. They would provide the hearing aid testing and delivery services, and we would be the provider of record. Of course, we followed the proper protocol, including getting them their own sub-provider number registered under our company.

In this case, we had established protocols and systems, but lacked manpower in certain parts of the state. We created a partnership with other businesses, using our systems and knowledge as leverage. Eventually, this system became cumbersome with size, and we found it more efficient to send our own employees and establish branch offices in certain areas. Until we reached that point, the joint ventures allowed us to expand rapidly with less capital than fast growth usually requires.

What is the key to a successful joint venture? It is utilizing the principle mentioned in the previous chapter, popularized by Sun Tzu in *The Art of War*, and used in business plans as the SWOT analysis: strengths, weaknesses, opportunities, and threats.

In the case of joint ventures, you need to understand the SWOT of both your own company, and that of your potential partner. When you can develop a plan that uses your strengths, and find a strategic partner that has strengths that compensate for your weaknesses, you have a good match.

Let's take an Internet example. If you have a product or service that has great value, but you don't have a long, developed customer list to market it to, you have a perfect setup for an endorsed mailing. You can start searching for someone who has an e-mail newsletter, e-zine, or blog with a large client base that would benefit from your product. You can develop a relationship with the owner or publisher, and ultimately set up a joint venture with him. He can market and promote your product or service to the people on his list, not as the originator, but as a believer who is endorsing and recommending it to his "tribe" or followers.

You benefit by being able to market to his clients and receive new orders from his endorsement. He benefits by offering a product his clients will appreciate and use, and he shares a percentage of the sales.

There is a real estate term that I really like. It is *highest and best use*. You might see a corner lot with a convenience store on it, but is that its highest and best use? Maybe a medical office building would be a better choice for that corner. Maybe a high rise condominium would provide a better return.

What is your highest and best use? What is the highest and best use of your enterprise? Rather than spending time and money on areas in which you or your business are not efficient, why not focus on your highest and best use and form strategic partnerships with companies that excel at the functions in which you do not excel?

Eventually, I realized my highest and best use wasn't in the hearing aid industry, but in innovative business creation and development. We spun off the portion of the business that was innovating and marketing our hearing aid company and created BestSellingExperts.com. It contains an Internet marketing and traffic generation firm, a book publishing and author coaching firm, and my own speaking and consulting services to show other small business owners ways to innovate, thrive, and survive, and how to position themselves as experts in their field.

There are many things you could consider leveraging. What are your personal strengths or your greatest abilities? What activities bring you the most value and joy?

You can leverage your talents, your gifts, and your time. Rather than spending 80% of your time on areas of mediocrity, focus 80% of your time and talents on those skills that provide you with your highest and best use, and create joint ventures to leverage those talents.

Leverage Is Power

ACTION STEPS

1. Answer the following questions:
   a. What is the load or result you or your business wants to move?
   b. Which business or part of your business is the fulcrum that you plan to rest your lever on?
   c. What can you create, innovate, or use as the lever that will move your load quickly and easily?
   d. What is your highest and best use?
   e. What is the highest and best use of your enterprise?
2. Review the list of potential levers, and then create a list of your own. There are many things you could consider leveraging.
   a. What are your personal strengths or your greatest abilities?
   b. What activities bring you the most value and joy?

REMEMBER

- When you use leverage, small changes can produce big results.
- Leverage can be created by the use of three items: a fulcrum, a load, and an applied force.
- If considering joint venture partners, you need to understand the SWOT of both your own company, and that of your potential partner. When you can develop a plan that uses your strengths, and find a strategic partner whose strengths compensate for your weaknesses, you have a good match.
- Focus on your highest and best use and form strategic partnerships with companies that excel at the functions in which you do not excel.

CHAPTER TEN

Mileposts and Pit Stops

T he Daytona 500 is a 500-mile-long race held every year in Florida. Imagine if you were planning to make a 500-mile trip. Now add high speed, curves, and intense competition. In today's environment, running a business can be better compared to the Daytona 500 than a leisurely 500-mile drive!

In 2011, Trevor Bayne became the youngest winner in the history of the Daytona 500. It required skill, focus, and intention to succeed. It also required a great team, which he had, as he was racing for one of the oldest and greatest teams in NASCAR, The Woods Brothers.

A race provides an excellent analogy for running a business. They both require planning, foresight, and investment before they even begin. Once the race does begin, the success of the driver depends on the team just as much as his own skills. Constant attention has to be paid to all the metrics—speed, temperature, tires, and fluid levels. Pit stops can be scheduled, but sometimes they must be taken unexpectedly. The winners are not lucky. They earn their wins by working hard for them.

We've already talked about a lot of the necessary concepts in previous chapters, such as vision, research, and creating a good team. Now I'd like to introduce some additional concepts.

One subject that isn't discussed much in today's business world is the need to pace yourself. Sure, in the early days of a new venture, it is normal and sometimes necessary to burn the midnight oil, but that has to be limited to the first part of the race while you find your place. Soon after the initial sprint, you need to pace yourself to prevent burnout.

We've heard about medical residents or new attorneys working 100 hours per week to meet the expectations of their superiors. Those are both mostly externally imposed schedules. As an entrepreneur, much of our drive is internal. Without some sort of governing mechanism, it is way too easy to burn yourself out.

Remember, most burnout occurs when CEOs and entrepreneurs are doing too much of the 80% of activities that should be delegated or deleted. At least as an entrepreneur, you have the ability to call the shots, and select what activities are most important for you to be doing at any particular time.

Whom should you compete with? Compete with yourself. Not on how many hours you can work, but how productive and effective you can be with your time and energy. Compete with your output of creative ideas from the previous week. Compete and increase the number of hours spent each day working on your top priority items.

There are times when it will help to ask for advice from the outside. A good board of advisors that you respect and trust is a great place to start. If you have a business coach, schedule regular meetings to get her outlook and to let her help you see your business from a distance, instead of right in the middle of it.

Mileposts are points on the way to achieving your goals and your vision. Even if you feel like it will take years to accomplish your vision, you need to log mileposts on a regular basis to show your team and yourself that you are making progress. These mileposts will confirm that you are heading in the right direction and on the path that will take you where you want to go.

The chapters of this book are placed in a significant order. Too many entrepreneurs stop themselves short of achieving their vision because they don't set their goals and mileposts, using the following sequence:

1. Establish your Vision—Chapter 1 is placed first, because this is the "long reach" purpose that you need to establish in the beginning

2. Plan—just like an architect, plan your strategy, taking both time and money into consideration
3. Execute your start-up in the right manner, as outlined in chapter 3
4. Develop your marketing strategy
5. Put your team in place; engage and motivate them
6. Create your culture by design, based on your values
7. Get the machine in motion by motivating your team, both emotionally and rationally
8. Set up a metrics system to measure and chart your progress
9. Leverage all your assets: people, knowledge, and your own strengths
10. Set up your mileposts, with precision. You now have a track record, a team, and a machine. Challenge yourself and your team to achieve performance-based goals on yearly, quarterly, and monthly schedules.

Remember to establish rewards and celebrations which occur as you and your team achieve the mileposts you set. Success will bring you closer together, and you will be better prepared for even greater challenges and celebrations.

Too many businesses set mileposts based on hope or greed. By completing steps one through ten, you can generate your mileposts based on the system you have created, and support it with your values and culture.

Pit stops are places where you can stop and check the tires and gauges. They give you the opportunity to make sure that everything you are doing is congruent with where you want to go, with your values, and with your vision.

Here are some gauges that I like to check. They were written by one of the richest men the world has ever seen:

King Solomon - paraphrased
- There is a lot of safety in having a number of good business advisors. Proverbs 11:14

  What are my advisors saying?
- Know where you are headed, and you'll stay on solid ground. Proverbs 4:25-26

  Are you on track with your plan?
- If you do the right thing, honesty will be your guide. But if you are crooked, you will be trapped by your own dishonesty. Proverbs 11:3

  Are your actions based on your rewards, or on your values?
- Try to find work you enjoy. It is a great gift if you do. Ecclesiastes 5:19

  Are we having fun yet?

Whether you take solace in following principles from the Bible, as I do, or from some other great book or person that you trust, it is important to have a solid moral compass that you believe in. Check your actions with your belief system often. Financial success is not a happy ending if you can't sleep well because you had to compromise your beliefs to achieve it.

If you created a list of values that you truly believe your company will do best to operate by, then your team members need to be consulted from time to time. The more familiar they are with what you value, the better they will be at making good decisions. I've had team members ask me if some action we were discussing went along with the company values we had established. We have, in some cases modified policies or changed plans to make sure we were being true to the values we had established.

There are rules to any game. I believe business is one of the best intellectual sports available. One of the great things about business is that the entrepreneur gets the opportunity to help create the rules of their particular game. Once established, play by your own rules, and your team will have an example to guide them.

The Power of Priority

ACTION STEPS

1. Increase the number of hours spent each day working on your top priority items
2. Log mileposts on a regular basis
3. Establish rewards and celebrations which occur as you and your team achieve the mileposts you set
4. Check your actions against the list of values which you chose to operate your company by

REMEMBER

- Soon after the initial sprint, you need to pace yourself to prevent burnout.
- Most burnout occurs when CEOs and entrepreneurs are doing too much of the 80% of activities that should be delegated or deleted.
- Mileposts are points on the way to achieving your goals and your vision.

- If you created a list of values that you truly believe your company will do best to operate by, then your team members need to be consulted from time to time.

CHAPTER ELEVEN

Staying
in Control

Money, capital, cash, savings, investments, inheritance, family loans, bank loans, SBA loans, bonds, convertible bonds, venture capital, angel investors, supplier financing... All of these financing terms, and more, seem to be floating in the air and in your mind, at the beginning of a new venture.

The fact of the matter is that you may be putting too much emphasis on some of these financing options at the wrong stage of your business. Let's look at four stages of a business and see what priorities should be the highest at each stage.

1. The start-up stage

    Every new entrepreneur is faced with the question "How much start-up capital do I have"? Sure, it's important to know the answer to that question, and it's certainly beneficial to have sufficient start-up capital. Having too much capital available, however, can lead to poor financial decisions and wasted money. There is something that is more important than cash in the early days of the company. Your priority should be sales.

Sales are the lifeblood of a new company. One of the most important reasons to prioritize sale is to establish proof of concept. You may believe that you have a great idea which will generate a high demand in the marketplace. But the real proof that your concept is sound comes when people reach for their wallets and commit to a purchase. Before you invest too much money, too much time, and too much of your energy into a new business, you should prove to yourself and to your present or future investors that you really do have a marketable, desirable, and well-received product or service.

Many businesses, especially those started by a solo entrepreneur, have survived the first stage purely due to the passion, belief, and intensity that were invested by the founder. Whether you're starting by yourself or with a team, with little start-up capital or with a lot, there's a lot to be said for the value of focusing purely on sales in the beginning.

Consider the initial growth created in the dot. com industry before the bubble burst in the late 1990s. New start-ups often had almost all the start-up money they wanted, usually more than they needed. What they didn't have were sales. Often they had no idea how they were going to monetize their project. A few, like Google, found a way and succeeded beyond their founders' dreams.

But the majority of the dot.com start-ups collapsed long before their sales approached significance.

If you're in the start-up stage, focus on sales. It's better to have the problem of so many sales that you are struggling to fulfill them all, than to have a lot of capital but little productive work to assign to your team because you have no or few sales.

2. The "let's roll" stage

Great! The company is off the ground. Sales are rolling in. Now is the time when "cash is king." Sales are your first priority during the start-up phase of the first six to twelve months. Once the machine has proven that it's going to work, it's important to have the cash to keep the machine well oiled. Where too much cash may have been wasted on ill-advised expenses and investments the first year, now you're beginning to see more clearly what buttons need to be pushed and what levers need to be pulled.

You are better served by having planned in advance for where the cash will go when the cash comes. Not having more capital than you need in the very beginning helps you to avoid waste and increases efficiency. But now you know your business model will work. Now is when you need to bring in the cash. Focus especially on your best usage of leverage. Keep your expenses lean, keep the sales rolling in, and if you need more cash, find a way to bring it in.

3. Growing up

The second stage of your business, when cash is king, typically takes you to year four or five. You may have heard the statistic that about 85% to 90% of all businesses fail during the first five years. Most people assume that's because of a lack of capital. Even though access to plenty of money may have helped, sometimes it just postpones the failure of the business a few years.

One of the main reasons businesses fail in the early years, in my opinion, is because the business grows faster than the learning curve of the entrepreneur and his team will allow. Sales come first, cash is king in the second stage, and in the third stage, gross profit margins should be the major focus. To take a business with rapidly growing sales and enough cash to survive to the next level, requires new skills. Skills that will provide a sufficient gross profit margin that will cover capital needs, future investments, and at least break-even profitability are often more learned than natural.

This is where the new entrepreneur often fails. There's an area of resistance here, especially at the $2 million to $3 million annual revenue level, which often stops a business like a glass ceiling. Whenever you reach a point in a business that you've never been before, don't assume that you can go beyond that point without outside advice. You may be at the level where you need to bring in more knowledge or additional team members. We'll talk about that later in this chapter. For now, just realize that at this stage of the business, you need to have enough margin above the line to pay for your past debts, your future investments, and have enough of a margin to cover some unavoidable mistakes.

4. Maturity

    Maturity is the stage of business that most businesses never reach. At this point, priorities change. In Stage 1, sales are top priority. In Stage 2, cash is king. Stage 3 is where gross profits are your focus. Maturity, Stage 4, is the time to focus on net profits.

    A mature business has its systems well designed, and its team well developed. Now is the time that the business should be running like a well-designed timepiece. High-growth becomes less important. Net profits should be the reward—the return on all of your investments of time, money, and emotional energy.

5. Growth and Change

    Just as your capital needs change during the growth of your business, so will a lot of others. You realize that your staff will grow. One mistake that is often made is trying to manage too many people. The beginning rule of thumb is that no one person should have more than seven people reporting to him or her.

    That means after your first seven employees, you need to start adding managers. Think of the three areas of business that form the three legs of the stool that we talked about in chapter 5. Those three critical areas were vision, marketing, and finance. You might consider which of those you are strongest in, and continue to manage those people yourself, for now. Make your first two managers ones that are strong in the other two strength areas you need help in. Eventually you will want to promote yourself, and hire one manager for each of the three legs.

There is a fine balance you will have to develop to keep yourself from being sucked into becoming just another worker. In one of my earlier companies, I hit a glass ceiling at $500,000 in annual sales because I had built a "job" around myself. I was so busy working in the business that I had no time to work on it. If you find yourself in that position, I would recommend reading *The E-Myth Revisited*, by Michael Gerber (Harper Collins, 1995).

After selling that business and breaking free, in my next company, I found myself slowly getting sucked into a position of being the key employee in one area after another. This time I was aware of the danger. Every time I realized I was filling a role that could be better handled by someone earning less than what I was worth as CEO, I would replace myself. At one point, after a period of rapid growth, I realized I spent most of my time dealing with suppliers, paying bills, and doing payroll. I hired a CFO even though I wasn't sure I could afford to do so. Despite my initial concern, it quickly became apparent it had been a great decision. Once I had time to become the CEO again, and focus on vision, growth, and networking, the company resumed expanding and growing.

Remember, no one person should have more than seven direct reports. When you have a number of managers reporting to you, it becomes necessary to create a level I call the executive team. Often your executives can be recruited from your managers; sometimes they need to come from outside your organization, particularly if you are at a level of growth that your managers have never experienced. At this point, you should only have three people reporting to you: the CEO, CFO, and VP of marketing, or whatever titles you have given the executives in those positions.

Remember also that you need to have more key team members than those reporting to you. You need an external team of advisors to keep you in balance. These would include your banker, attorney, business coach, accountant, and board of advisors.

Finally, if you expect to remain in control of your time and your life, you need to remember to be balanced in all areas. You are more than just a business machine. You need to include family time, personal time, spiritual development time, time for your friends, and time for personal growth and knowledge. Time spent away from your business, whether at conferences or just resting and relaxing, is not wasted. Rather than time management, think of this as energy management.

Staying in control sometimes means giving control to others, and empowering them while you take a break. It's a great experience when your business develops to the point that you can take a few weeks off and return to higher sales, without much to do except go through the mail that has accumulated. To stay in control of your own life, learn to delegate control to others!

Sustainable
Power

ACTION STEPS

1. Make sales your priority in order to establish proof of concept
2. Plan in advance for where the cash will go when the cash comes in
3. Once you know your business model will work, it's time to bring in the cash
4. Cultivate skills that will provide a sufficient gross profit margin to cover capital needs, future investments, and at least break-even profitability
5. After your first seven employees, start adding managers

REMEMBER

- Before you invest too much money, time, and energy into a new business, prove to yourself and to investors that you have a marketable, desirable, and well-received product or service.

- Where too much cash may have been wasted on ill-advised expenses and investments the first year, after you have survived the start-up phase, you'll see more clearly what buttons need to be pushed and what levers need to be pulled.

- In Stage 1, sales are top priority. In Stage 2, cash is king. Stage 3 is where gross profits are your focus. Maturity, Stage 4, is the time to focus on net profits.

- No one person should have more than seven direct reports.

CHAPTER TWELVE

Legacy

What you are about to learn could double your retirement nest egg. It could prevent disaster. Start learning these concepts now. Planning ahead can create a fortune for you, instead of disappointment.

Everyone needs an exit plan. Everyone. To begin with, it's a proven fact that we are all going to exit. And the timing of us leaving this life is usually not planned. Unless you have a continuation strategy in place, the government or the courts will make those decisions for you. And if you want to sell your business, the best time to prepare for it is sooner rather than later.

If you sell your business, planning ahead can make an amazing difference in your selling price. The amount you receive is often based on a multiple of net profits. Let's say someone offers you a selling price of five times your yearly net profit (5x net). That might be tempting. But it could also be disappointing, if your accounting is handled the way many small business owners manage their books.

Most of us try to avoid taxes. One way to pay fewer taxes now is to prevent your business from showing a profit. There are legal ways to expense purchases at an accelerated rate, to write off now rather than later. The problem is by expensing now to avoid taxes you decrease the amount that could be used to give your business a higher valuation.

Right, I know. You're not planning to sell soon, or ever. You'd rather save on taxes, and worry about selling when you are ready to retire. But the unexpected happens every day. That $100,000 write off that would save you a $30,000 tax bill will cost you $500,000 based on a multiple of 5 times net. In other words, without proper planning, you are gambling. The cost of a great tax planner can become insignificant in comparison to the savings they can create.

What about your vision? Will the transfer or sale of your business—whether because of moving on to a new interest, retirement, or illness— fit in with your vision for it, for you, and for your company?

What about the values you so carefully established? If you end up having to sell your business because of health, relationships, or any of the many possible reasons, the sale or the aftermath may not be in line with your values, if you do not plan ahead.

If you are selling, should it be on your own, or through a business broker? What are the tax consequences? As you can see, there are a lot of major questions that require either a lot of research, or a very knowledgeable friend. Although this will be a short chapter, let me simplify a few things for you.

Fifty Ways to Leave Your Business?

I know I date myself by telling you that I was in high school when Paul Simon's "Fifty Ways to Leave Your Lover" was a hit song. Fortunately, you don't have to consider that many possibilities if you are thinking of selling your business now, or way in the future. Here are four ways that cover most of the possibilities:

1. Sell to family members
2. Sell to co-owners or partners
3. Sell to your employees
4. Sell to an outside third party

See, it's not so complicated! You can potentially look over the four choices above, and immediately see which might be the most likely route for you to take. There are inherent pros and cons to each choice, so do your research and talk with advisors.

Another subject to talk to an attorney or advisor about is a business continuity document. You need to make plans now for how your business will continue to operate if something unexpected happens to you. The business continuity document spells out that plan.

Just like it is unfair to a wife and children to not have life insurance or a plan in place in case of your accidental death, it is also very sad if spouses, children, partners, and employees are left holding that bag in regards to your business. If something untoward happens to you, who will pay the bills? What about payroll? What about all those things that only you do?

My daughter has a friend whose husband had a successful construction company. When he died unexpectedly at a young age, she thought she knew enough about it to take it over and run it. Unfortunately, successful entrepreneurship requires mastering a multitude of skills which are usually developed on the way to creating a successful business. She did not survive the first year in business.

So not only did a young mother have to deal with the grief over the loss of her husband, she also ran into the brick wall of running a business beyond her level of competency. That led to the further heartaches of business failure, bankruptcy, loss of income, loss of home, and the sorrow of seeing the support for all the employees' families end. All of this happened within a short period of time. This is a tragedy that should have been avoided!

Don't let a tragedy like this affect you or someone you know in business. You can take steps not only to make your own ventures successful, but you can be an ambassador and spread the word. Start with your own business.

Create a
Powerful
Legacy

ACTION STEPS

1. Get an independent third-party business valuation
2. Continue to build your team
3. Continue to motivate your key players
4. Research the tax laws—talk to an accountant
5. Create an exit plan, whether for now or down the road
6. Have a business continuity plan drawn up
7. Create a personal financial game plan
8. Include trusted advisors in the process above

REMEMBER

- An integral part of your strategic planning process is creating a detailed plan of your personal exit, whether planned or unexpected.

Epilogue

Throughout your life, you will come to crossroads. These are places where you are able to choose a new path to travel on.

You are at one right now. For most people, their future is determined by their past. They become so entangled in the present, they never take the time to pull up to the 30,000 foot level and look at the forest. All they see is the trees all around them.

This book is intended to take you to that big picture level. Don't close your eyes. Take a realistic look at where you've been, and where you are now. Then don't just do the same thing. It's time to choose a different path, one that will take you to a different destination.

You've got a game plan in your hand. Go back to the chapter headings at the beginning of this book. Review them, and decide if you have worked through each area to your satisfaction. Check off the areas that you need to work on, and then schedule a half day at a time to come up with a plan to handle each area.

I had an awesome revelation about determination, passion, and love when I was around 12 years old that I'll never forget. My father was not a demonstrative man, and rarely expressed his love for his family verbally.

I was amazed at my father's tenacity in going to work as a carpenter. Whether it was during the middle of an Iowa spring thunderstorm or a blizzard in January, he would get in his truck and drive the 50 miles each way to get to work. Driving to work in such extreme weather seemed foolish to me, until I had the realization that was his expression of his love for his family. Direct verbal expression is the most effective way to communicate love; however, his drive had an admirable motivation.

What drives you? What vision would make you get up early in the morning and drive through a blizzard to bring you closer to its accomplishment? Harness that passion. Let your vision be the basis for guiding you in your business and your life. Amazing feats can be accomplished when you focus your energy on reaching a vision that has become your motivator, the dream that fuels your actions.

Nothing happens until you choose it, and take action on it. Start today, and do it now*!*

About the Author

**Bob Bare** is an author, speaker and founder of BestSellingExperts.com, a Texas based integrated media company and online community committed to assist companies and individuals in branding, broadcasting and living their vision through Expert Positioning, Publishing, Publicity and Public Speaking.

A serial entrepreneur with 40 years of wisdom to share, Bob is known for his ability to create, grow and turn around a successful multi-million dollar business while keeping his vision and values in sight.

An Iowa native, Bob lives in Dallas, Texas, with Jan, his wife of over 30 years. He is the proud father of 3 children and grandfather of 6. He enjoys giving back to his community through active leadership roles in his local church and Rotary club.

In an effort to pay it forward, Bob produces and hosts Experts Weekly radio, publishes the BestSelling Experts Weekly newsletter and mentors start-up entrepreneurs.

For more information about Bob's books, coaching programs and live training, please visit BobBare.com and be sure to connect through the social media icons on the homepage.

Resource Guide

I. FREE RESOURCES

The tools below will aid you and provide clarity in implementing the action steps offered by Bob in each chapter. You can download them completely free of charge by visiting www.MorePowerBook.com/free or scanning the QR code to get direct access from your mobile phone.

What's Your Vision? What's Your Culture (Worksheet)
Sample Editable Business Plan
Competitive Analysis For Your Business
Essential Keys To Franchising by Paul Miltonberger
Sample Employee Personality Assessment
Leverage is Power - Expert Video by Bob Bare
Start-Up Financial Kit

II. ENHANCED AUDIO VERSION OF MORE POWER

Bring More Power! to your commute or morning jog. Enjoy the simple and powerful principles that guarantee lasting success in any business and take advantage of additional content provided by Bob Bare: stories, expert quotes and interviews.

For more information and to order your copy, please visit http://morepower.com/audio or scan the QR code with your smart phone.

III. MORE POWER TO YOU!

In this 10 week LIVE Telecast, Bob will coach you through the powerful principles he shares in More Power! so you can easily implement them FAST and get your questions answered.

Here's what you will learn how to:

1. Make More Money And Get More Power Through Vision
2. Plan For More Power
3. Start-up or Restructure Your Business With Power
4. Achieve More Marketing Power

5. Build A More Powerful Team
6. Take Advantage of The Power of Culture
7. Motivate With Power
8. Measure Your Power
9. Leverage Yourself With Power
10. Make The Power Of Priority Work For You
11. Attain Sustainable Power
12. Create A Powerful Legacy

To learn more and to register for this limited-time, limited-seat event, please visit http://morepower.com/forward or scan the QR code with your smart phone.

Nothings change unless something moves. Get moving!

Printed in the USA
CPSIA information can be obtained
at www.ICGtesting.com
JSHW082356140824
68134JS00020B/2101